McKean's Mills

VIVIAN GARNER

Copyright © 2017 Vivian Garner

All rights reserved.

ISBN-13: 978-1981760015

Published by Immortalise
www.immortalise.com.au

Written by Vivian Garner
Email: garnervivian@dodo.com.au

McKean's Mills

That's what it was still called when I was old enough to read a map of Grey County. It's not now, of course; a school, a few houses and a timber mill don't qualify any more. But then it was important and not just for Andrew and Lizzie McKean. The mill provided both timber and employment. The school was the only one for miles so the kids came. And the teacher boarded at Lizzie's across the road.

Contents

The Mountain 1

PROGENITORS 3

Lizzie 3

Andrew 9

THEIR CHILDREN 13

Beatrice 13

Clunis 15

GL 20

Nellie 23

Annie 25

Lost Two 27

OUR HOUSE 28

Our house … 29

Homecoming 33

Andrew and Lizzy 35

Seven Children 35

McKean's Mills

The Mountain

Town was where we lived
but 'the mountain' was where we came from.
We hadn't moved far — fifteen miles all downhill —
and we went back weekends to my great grandparents.
Andrew and Lizzie had a houseful
as on sunny summers we gathered on their lawn:
Clunis' kids, Beatrice's kids,
sometimes the city cousins.
Lizzie got us picking dandelions
while the adults chattered.
I thought she was just keeping us busy;
I didn't know about the wine.
Sometimes we went into the kitchen
and Lizzie put out bread and jam.
She made her own butter and it was yellow–orange:
too strong for me. The jam was good,
elderberry sometimes, a bit seedy.

Vivian Garner

I could walk the sugar bush unsupervised,

pick leeks — and trilliums.

They've been canonized, trilliums.

You don't pick them any more: they're symbolic.

In town I was kept close, an only child,

but I could wander on the mountain.

Nothing here to hurt you, they said.

That's changed now:

bears and wolves and cougars —

dropped in to put back the natural balance, they say.

They expropriated 'the mountain', you see;

it's called an escarpment now, and a park.

Not all of it; not Lizzie's place.

The cousins have that.

McKean's Mills

PROGENITORS

Lizzie

The barn slumps slowly from the weight of white winters
    past
but I remember sunny summers:
laughter in the hay loft, tossing feed down for the cow,
eggs and flying feathers and the angry rooster,
Diamond's stall pungent and the wagon waiting.
No manure pile for Andrew, not near the house;
the hillock by the maple bush grew each spring.

Later, Lizzie and her lantern, tossing hay
on her lonely nightly roaming,
frightening the neighbours —
fearful of the fire that never came.

Vivian Garner

The barn was Lizzie's:
the cow, the hens, the hay mow. Diamond had a stall
    there,
        hauled the sleigh for winter logging
        and summer timber from Andrew's mill to town,
but Andrew and Diamond were under orders in the barn.

In the attic above the kitchen,
hired for the mill, men slept.

Upstairs
   schoolteacher's bedroom
      and the family: five children, Andrew, visitors.
Downstairs
   Lizzie's mother had the room off the parlour.
   Lizzie slept on the kitchen daybed,
      childbearing over,
little Russell drowned and a baby born dying — enough.

McKean's Mills

Lizzie fed them all
   with the hens,
   the garden Diamond ploughed for her every spring,
   the orchard, the stubborn red necked Guernsey,
   bush-found leeks and blackberries.
Even the dandelions made wine for winter ills.
My mom and dad found that wine later, after Lizzie left.
Thought to have a little 'warm up' and had to stop the
   night.
Lindsay, her youngest living,
died old with the marks of Lizzie's sewing still on his
   knee
   where he sliced it on the chaff cutter.
She had practised on battered hens and a wounded calf or
   two;
town was a long way by horse.

Vivian Garner

We spent a summer there, Grandma and I.

Grandpa came on weekends.

Lizzie and Andrew off to California to see Lindsay;

   the last time for Andrew.

Me swinging on a gate, stung by a bee,

Grandma mixed the bicarb

     pasted on my cheek.

Grandpa fleeing the orchard,

rooster attacking his shoulder.

Grandma knew to smack it —

but Grandpa was a townie.

Grandpa's smile, whetting the hatchet;

it made tough soup — but we ate it anyway.

Lizzie lived with us later,

argued with the women:

   my mom, my aunt, Grandma;

ate ice cream at night with Grand-dad,

Grandma disapproving.

McKean's Mills

My dad brought her offerings:
brandy in a bottle for her eggnog —
for her heart, she said.

Two ancient swains in the kitchen sipping tea,
Lizzie crowned with her white braids, her purple dress,
    blue eyes alight.
She's Lizzie Lang, you know. Prettiest girl on the
    mountain.
They said it every Saturday.
Grandma disapproved.
Lizzie was her mother.

Grandma planned a holiday.
'The home' was booked;
they called it respite.
Lizzie took to her room.

When they went to get her
she had left by the window.

Vivian Garner

It was five feet to the ground.
Lizzie phoned home from the cousins' —
 she'd be back when they were.

Lizzie was in her nineties before 'the home' finally got
    her
— but not for long.

Andrew

They named the place after him:
McKean's Mills.
It was on the map — once.
We liked to look it up
until 'the mountain' became an escarpment
and part national park
and they made new maps.
Mostly I know what they told me.
I guess most of it was true.

His big mill had burned down before I was born —
set alight by a disgruntled employee,
they said.
All I remember is the stone chimney
and the pictures.
It had a tall, tall smokestack
and there were no cranes then.
He put it up from underneath,

Vivian Garner

one piece shoved into the one above
until it was high enough for Andrew.

Once he broke down on the way to town
    with a load behind Diamond,
and a shattered gear.
He sat by the road
and carved a new one from hard timber,
 refusing offers of help.

I remember him at the one-man mill he built later.
He clamped the logs to his travel and rode up and down
    with them,
turning them for the saw with a giant hook
as the slabs fell away.
He built the engine himself; ran the travel on old used
    railway tracks.
The boiler fire was fed with the sawdust
and the water came from the creek.

McKean's Mills

There was a giant handle I loved to pump
and watch the old fire hose fill.
Though I was little, it moved easy.
Andrew was good at making things work.
The slabs heated the house;
the acres fed Diamond and the red necked Guernsey.
The outhouse fertilized the orchard.
Lizzie's garden and kitchen did the rest.

Younger, he was a business man
and stayed at the best hotel on his trips to town:
dinner with proper white cloths and crystal;
merchandise delivered, payment received.
He stayed overnight, sometimes a few nights,
especially after Lizzie moved downstairs.

Later, Andrew had a car — the first on the mountain —
and drove it with one hand on the horn
    straight down the middle,

Vivian Garner

up and down the gravelled ridges

where later I learned to drive.

Keep over, you can't see who's coming.

Not Andrew.

He didn't talk easily when I was around.

He hurt his leg and needed an operation

so he stayed at our place

in the living room on a hospital bed.

They told him his days on the mountain were over

but he was healthy for his age;

he would recover nicely.

He said nothing but his face turned to stone.

McKean's Mills

THEIR CHILDREN

Beatrice

She was adored by Andrew,

the oldest of the five,

walked 15 miles to town for the dance

and home in the morning — uphill.

She was just 'Grandma' to me

and I never thought of her as old or young.

We went everywhere together

until I started school.

It seemed right, the CWA meetings

where I recited and showed off what she taught me:

I could list countries, their capitals and prime ministers.

The local Liberal party, the CWA, the WCTU,

even the 'Home and School':

long after her children were grown

Grandma dominated them all.

Vivian Garner

She was religious and attended church,
but she never denied its flaws
or stayed out of its politics.
I was more convinced than converted
but she gave me the best that she knew.
The family business served her well:
she bought wholesale locally,
sent the goods to 'the shop' — and the bills.
She liked quality —
regularly took the train to the city to find it.
She had good credit. Grandpa always paid.
She planned and plotted and mostly got her way
in family affairs until Grandpa died.

The business went to other hands.
She had an allowance,
sat in a chair in a corner,
her resentment tucked close.
They hired a companion.
It didn't help.

Clunis

They forced him off the road, three overgrown
        larrikins,
vigour and youth uncontrolled.
It was to be a bit of fun:
scare the old man, rock the car, yell,
maybe get him out and watch him run.
It was Hallowe'en, a great excuse:
roughhouse version of trick, no treat.

We had a lot of it then.
Hallowe'en in the country meant
finding the outhouse moved, sometimes too late;
taking a .22 to the few street lights,
the local cop following, replacing the bulbs as he went.
Boys would be boys.

Vivian Garner

Townies settled for soaping windows
and grabbing a little kid's bag of treats.
The older of us shrugged and ignored them,
got on with the good stuff:
kids in costumes and candy apples,
popcorn and home made fudge,
neighbour waiting at the door.
Only the grumps left the porch light off.

Plaid shirt, jeans and little brother's
six shooters in holsters;
disguise enough for the high school dance.
Some took it serious and came as robots
or clowns in face masks, leaving us guessing.
Sometimes they were the teachers,
supervising incognito.

It was dangerous, that Hallowe'en,
forcing Clunis off the road.
Clunis was over 70, wrinkled, little and lean.

McKean's Mills

They expected him to plead, to run.
They wanted him scared.
They cheered when he slipped from the car,
ready for the chase.

He ran straight for them,
swinging a rubber hose.
They needed stitches and one had a broken bone.
They didn't know Clunis.

He drove every day, pacers and trotters;
he raced on the sulky and held his place.
Clunis understood a whip and he understood tight
       places.

The parents sued, seeing only young bodies marked.
The judge asked Clunis why he kept a hose.
To siphon fuel for the tractor.
It was case dismissed and lesson learned.

Vivian Garner

Clunis, my grandmother's brother,

grew potatoes in the front field

and kept a practice track around the outside.

He had 14 kids, kept a farm

and trained horses. He raced his own,

and trained the best in the country.

He was a silent man, answered with a grin

or a headshake,

    before he turned and walked away.

I never knew him until he grew very old.

We sat in the front parlour;

the family were gathered after a funeral.

Clunis had come late — had a mare to look after.

He told me how he'd arrived after dark

    and the foal had run out to meet him,

    eyes shining in the headlights,

    brand new and still birthing wet.

Prettiest thing I ever saw.

The wonder was still on him.

McKean's Mills

His family smiled as they told me
      about Clunis and the court case.
They sure underestimated the old man.

I understood the 14 kids then,
how they grew the way they did:
good folks, family folks, looking after each other.
Great cousins.
I had wondered if they felt loved.
I learned they had felt protected.

Vivian Garner

GL

He was christened George Lindsay,
answered to Lindsay at home;
but once away he became GL.

GL was the youngest of Lizzie's brood,
the golden-skinned Californian
who made good.
It was party time when he flew home
and he smiled as he told us how safe it was
because they sold him a million-dollar-insurance
from a machine in the airport.

He was the youngest; Clunis was his older brother.
Clunis had dared him to climb naked
from their second-floor bedroom window and drop
into the snow below, then followed him, laughing.
They dared a lot.

McKean's Mills

He moved to town to his married sister's —
    my grandparents —
to get his high school.
Friends dared him to run naked
past the Baptist church on Sunday morning.
They called him 'Sam Slick from Pumpkin Crick'.

When he left for California no one wondered that
pretty Anica followed the golden boy.
Only later did we learn about the early birth.
Golden lives tarnished easily then
    but GL had the Midas touch in many things.

He was the first of us to fly
and he brought his mother back
a shimmering yellow housecoat.
Glamour and gold suited GL.
He aged well, stayed lean.
Anica kept him dressed in the latest style;
both liked to put on a show.

Vivian Garner

When he was 80 we all went out to dinner.
We were all flying then and
California was our winter vacation.
He came late; he was doing repairs, he said,
and had to get down off the roof.

His daughter grinned, whispered,
He's a show off. Jimmy was working.
He was just watching.

She adored him. We all did.

McKean's Mills

Nellie

Nellie came to us
a couple times a year;
hurried visits
but we expected that.

We did our city shopping from Nellie's.
She dispatched taxis as we ate,
with the two-way seldom silent
on the kitchen table.
She made hats —
plaster heads lined the sideboard.
At Christmas she worked night shift
in the post office.

Nellie married a man and a business.
Later, she joined a political party,
her husband chauffeured dignitaries,
the cars became limousines

and the drivers wore dress suits.

Nellie wore mink and shopped in New York.

There was always a place for us

on Brock Avenue

while Nellie lived there.

McKean's Mills

Annie

I have two photos.

In one,

me in front in a long pink dress

and curls past my shoulders,

with a basket of flowers,

slightly bewildered:

flower girl in a wedding party.

One of Annie's daughters was getting married.

In the background

the family:

Annie and Harold;

the bride and groom;

another son;

another daughter;

and the eldest, Jack, a pilot —

framed in the pride of his uniform

in a photo on the wall behind.

Vivian Garner

The other, much later:

Annie and Harold,

shrunken in age,

faded, almost transparent,

standing in front of a fireplace

with the two daughters and one son —

and on the wall behind,

Jack, framed in his uniform still,

ever young.

McKean's Mills

Lost Two

The sixth baby died in Grandma's arms.
Grandma was the eldest and Lizzie was cooking.
They knew it wouldn't live;
I never knew why.
I think it was a girl.
Grandma wouldn't say more.

Russell, Lizzie's seventh, died young.
Grandma found her baby brother
drowned in the cistern that held the house water.
His clothing was skirted as was the custom.
Grandma said it wasn't even wet through.
They all thought someone else had him
until too late.

Her parents kept separate bedrooms after that.

Vivian Garner

OUR HOUSE

Grandma married a businessman and lived in town. When Lizzie could no longer live on the mountain alone, Grandpa bought the place and kept it for her to visit, as it was, until she died. The cousins have it now.

We were a family. Grandpa's house in town was big, my parents had married and moved in upstairs in the aftermath of the depression and never left. My aunt lived with us and my uncle moved his family in for a time. Lizzie spent her last years with us after Andrew died.

When I married and left home, it was always where we came back to, eventually all seven of us. We didn't move in to stay but we never questioned our welcome. My parents kept the upstairs; Grandma lived downstairs until she needed to go into care.
It was my house, our house. It was where we belonged.

McKean's Mills

Our house ...

was big

with spaces to hide.

I hid a lot.

It was a full life house:

my house,

Grandpa's house, Grandma's pride.

Mom and Dad stayed in it

all their lives

which surprised Grandma and Grandpa.

Auntie B lived in it and kept me company

until Uncle John came along.

I was eleven then and I missed her.

Grandma had finally agreed:

we were going to share a room —

but B only slept in it the night before her wedding.

I moved in after.

I played piano for her to come down the stairs

and stand in front of the big bay windows.

I helped pass sandwiches to the crowd later.
My mother and my uncle Gerald had also married
    in front of those windows.
I didn't.

Uncle Gerald moved next door.
Grandpa owned the lot, you see.
They lived with us while the house was built,
three of them:
Uncle Gerald, Ella and Roger.
Roger was a pest.
I never had a brother and his baby sister didn't get born
    until after they had moved next door.
He had to do.
Roger and I played ping-pong on Grandma's dining
    table,
hid under it,
made forts out of the chesterfield cushions
and got on Great Grandma's nerves;
she lived with us too.

McKean's Mills

I remember Great Grandpa in the living room
on a hospital bed. He died soon after.
B slept in Mom's living room on Mom's couch.
I slept in Mom and Dad's big bedroom behind the
    dresser.
The city cousins came to visit
and took the room B and I wanted to share
until Grandma gave in.
I won. They lost.
We needed that room.

Christmas was fun.
Grandpa always chose his own tree early
from his own bush.
He let me help.
We put a ribbon on it and waited.
When Grandma said we could,
we took a sleigh and hauled it home.
It was always too tall.
Grandpa cut it off until it only touched the ceiling.

Vivian Garner

He drove nails into the woodwork to tie it to.
Grandma objected. Every year.
We closed the sliding doors on it and Grandma locked
 them. No peeking.
Roger and I hung the Christmas cards above the
 doorways
and thought the day would never come.

We all came to breakfast in Grandma's big kitchen —
from upstairs, downstairs, next door.
Grandpa crept up the front stairs for me
and we went down early, Christmas morning.
No presents till after breakfast:
Grandma's rules.
But there was always a doll on the tree
that Grandpa could just reach
and take down to see whose name was on it.
The stockings were fair game.
They had nuts and an orange and candy
and I never wanted breakfast.

McKean's Mills

Homecoming

I visit the cousins, call on old friends,
walk the historic main street,
get lost in the new suburbs,
and wonder where the creek went.

I stay away from my home street:
the chestnut trees are gone;
disease got them.
It's just a road.

I sold the house.
It's a B & B now they say.
We agree not to drive by.

Vivian Garner

At least 3 generations of McKeans built timber mills. The last one I know of was in Grey County, Ontario, Canada and the builder, Andrew McKean, was my great grandfather.

I write the stories as I remember them and as I have been told. They are memories, not history. They are my heritage as I carry it in my heart and as I have passed it on to my children.

Vivian Garner

Andrew and Lizzy

Andrew McKean was born October 10, 1867 – died Feb. 7, 1952

Elizabeth Catherine Lang (Lizzy) was born Feb. 15, 1865 – died Sept. 8, 1959

They were married April 17, 1894 and lived at McKean's Mills all their married lives until age brought them to town. Lizzy stayed at the mountain after Andrew died and continued to spend summers there.

Seven Children

Beatrice, 11 Nov. 1896

Alexnder CLUNIS 1898

Nellie 1899

Annie 1900

George LINDSAY 1901

Russell 1902

Evelyn 1904

The last two died young. The others went on to marry and their stories are mentioned but not complete here. The surviving five all had children. Clunis' family was especially large.

There are many McKean descendants around the Collingwood area and some as far away as California and Australia. There may be more not mentioned. I have not tried to number the direct descendants, I am sure the descendant families continue to grow, mine included. In this generation.I can add the 18 of my grandchildren, the great grandchildren continue to come. I can't speak for the others, some I keep in touch with, many I have met. Andrew and Lizzy are as far back as I can remember. There is a long family history but for me; this is where it begins.

A Family history 'The McKean Family' has been compiled for the family by Sandy Conn and Ruby Marlatt c1996

www.ingramcontent.com/pod-product-compliance
Lightning Source LLC
Chambersburg PA
CBHW072022290426
44109CB00018B/2318